WITHDRAWN

WELCOME TO THE U.S.A.
DELAWARE

Written by Ann Heinrichs   Illustrated by Matt Kania
Content Adviser: Andrea Gomez, Education Coordinator,
Historical Society of Delaware, Wilmington, Delaware

The Child's World

Published in the United States of America by The Child's World®
PO Box 326 • Chanhassen, MN 55317-0326
800-599-READ • www.childsworld.com

Photo Credits
Cover: Kevin Fleming/Corbis; frontispiece: Getty Images/Stone/Jake Rajs.

Interior: AP/Wide World Photo: 21 (Chris Gardner), 33 (Baltimore Sun/Kim Hairston); Nan Ciuffetelli: 17; Corbis: 9 (Scott T. Smith), 26 (William A. Bake); Delaware Office of Tourism: 13; Delaware State Parks: 6; Delmarva Poultry Industry: 25; Kevin Fleming/Corbis: 10, 18, 29, 30, 34; Mark E. Gibson/Corbis: 14, 22.

Acknowledgments
The Child's World®: Mary Berendes, Publishing Director

Editorial Directions, Inc.: E. Russell Primm, Editorial Director; Katie Marsico, Associate Editor; Judith Shiffer, Assistant Editor; Matt Messbarger, Editorial Assistant; Susan Hindman, Copy Editor; Melissa McDaniel, Proofreader; Kevin Cunningham, Peter Garnham, Matt Messbarger, Olivia Nellums, Chris Simms, Molly Symmonds, Katherine Trickle, Carl Stephen Wender, Fact Checkers; Tim Griffin/IndexServ, Indexer; Cian Loughlin O'Day, Photo Researcher and Editor

The Design Lab: Kathleen Petelinsek, Design; Julia Goozen, Art Production

Library of Congress Cataloging-in-Publication Data
Heinrichs, Ann.
  Delaware / by Ann Heinrichs ; cartography and illustrations by Matt Kania.
    p. cm. — (Welcome to the U.S.A.)
  Includes index.
  ISBN 1-59296-470-2 (library bound : alk. paper) 1. Delaware—Juvenile literature.
I. Kania, Matt, ill. II. Title.
  F164.3.H45 2005
  975.1—dc22   2005012081

Ann Heinrichs is the author of more than 100 books for children and young adults. She has also enjoyed successful careers as a children's book editor and an advertising copywriter. Ann grew up in Fort Smith, Arkansas, and lives in Chicago, Illinois.

**About the Author
Ann Heinrichs**

Matt Kania loves maps and, as a kid, dreamed of making them. In school he studied geography and cartography, and today he makes maps for a living. Matt's favorite thing about drawing maps is learning about the places they represent. Many of the maps he has created can be found in books, magazines, videos, Web sites, and public places.

**About the
Map Illustrator
Matt Kania**

On the cover: Go canoeing! Go hiking! Enjoy Delaware's natural beauty at Hoopes Reservoir.
On page one: Watch the bales of hay fly! Visit Odessa at harvest time!

OUR DELAWARE TRIP

Delaware's Nicknames: The First State, the Diamond State, the Blue Hen State, Small Wonder

WELCOME TO DELAWARE

Are you ready for a tour of Delaware? Just follow that loopy dotted line. It will lead you on some great adventures!

You'll explore sailing ships and water mills. You'll learn about shipwrecks and pirates. You'll roam the woods and picnic on the beach. And you'll watch pumpkins flying through the air!

That's just a taste of what's to come. There's much more to see and do. So let's not waste another minute. Just buckle up and hang on tight. We're off to Delaware!

As you travel through Delaware, watch for all the interesting facts along the way.

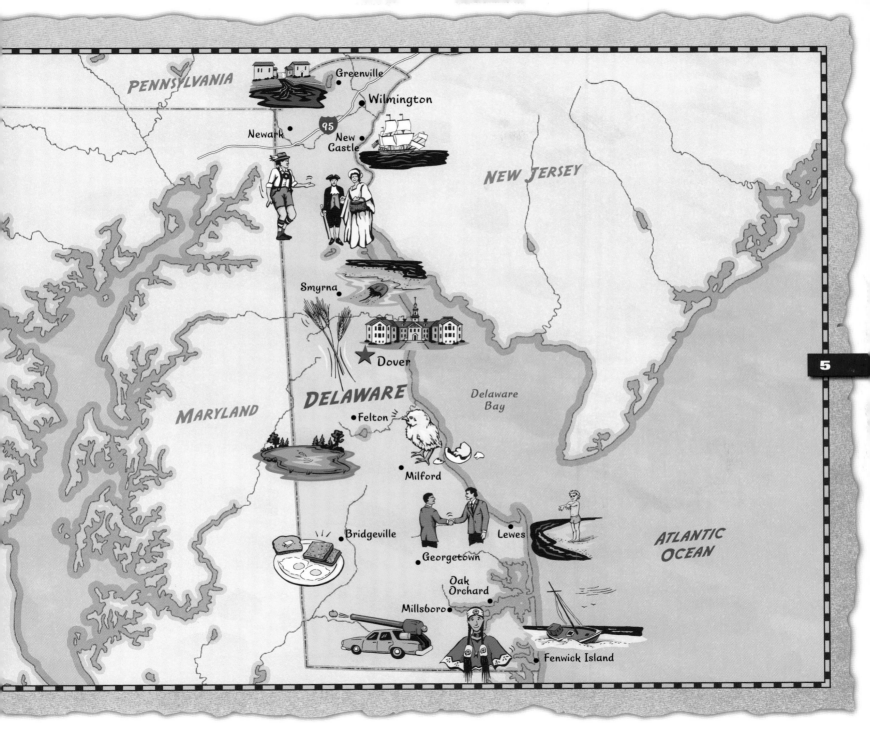

PENNSYLVANIA

Greenville

Wilmington

Newark

95

New
Castle

NEW JERSEY

Smyrna

Dover

MARYLAND

DELAWARE

Delaware
Bay

Felton

Milford

Bridgeville

Georgetown

Lewes

ATLANTIC
OCEAN

Oak
Orchard

Millsboro

Fenwick Island

The word *Delmarva* was made from the names of Delaware, Maryland, and Virginia.

How about a relaxing walk through scenic woods? Head to Killens Pond State Park!

6

Rhode Island is the only state that's smaller than Delaware.

Killens Pond State Park near Felton

Wander along the nature trail. Make your way through woodlands and fields. At last, you come to a sparkling pond. You're enjoying Killens Pond State Park!

Delaware is a tiny state. It's on the Delmarva **Peninsula.** It shares this peninsula with Maryland and Virginia. Many lakes and ponds are scattered around Delaware.

Delaware's whole eastern border faces water. The Delaware River is in the northeast. It flows into Delaware Bay. The bay then joins the Atlantic Ocean. Many beaches line Delaware's coast. The rest of the state is a low-lying plain.

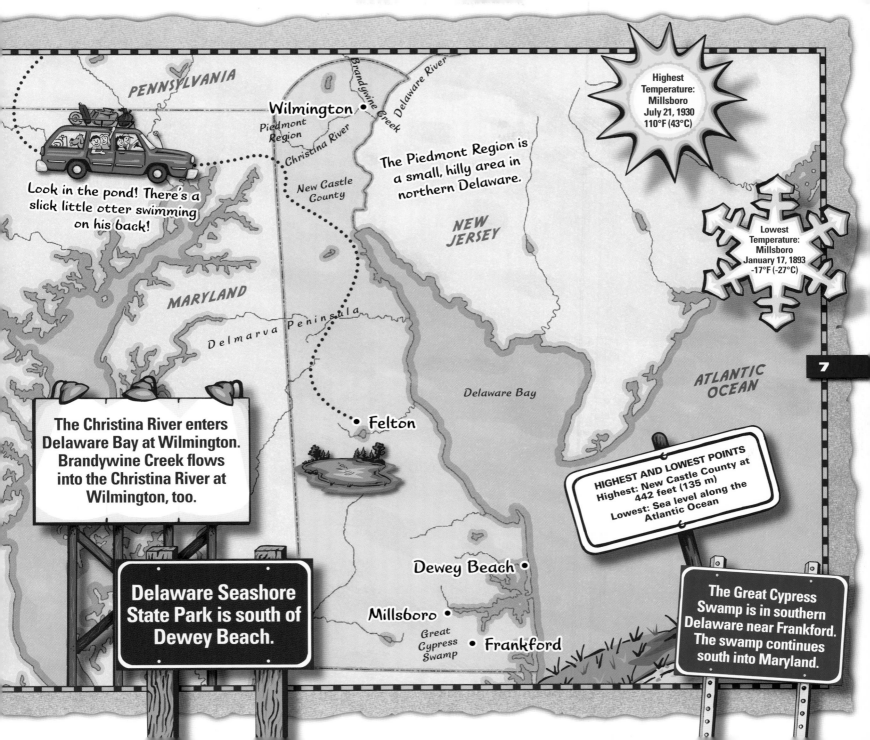

PENNSYLVANIA

Look in the pond! There's a slick little otter swimming on his back!

Wilmington

Piedmont Region

Brandywine Creek

Delaware River

Christina River

New Castle County

MARYLAND

Delmarva Peninsula

The Piedmont Region is a small, hilly area in northern Delaware.

NEW JERSEY

Highest Temperature: Millsboro July 21, 1930 110°F (43°C)

Lowest Temperature: Millsboro January 17, 1893 -17°F (-27°C)

ATLANTIC OCEAN

Delaware Bay

Felton

The Christina River enters Delaware Bay at Wilmington. Brandywine Creek flows into the Christina River at Wilmington, too.

HIGHEST AND LOWEST POINTS
Highest: New Castle County at 442 feet (135 m)
Lowest: Sea level along the Atlantic Ocean

Dewey Beach

Delaware Seashore State Park is south of Dewey Beach.

Millsboro

Great Cypress Swamp

Frankford

The Great Cypress Swamp is in southern Delaware near Frankford. The swamp continues south into Maryland.

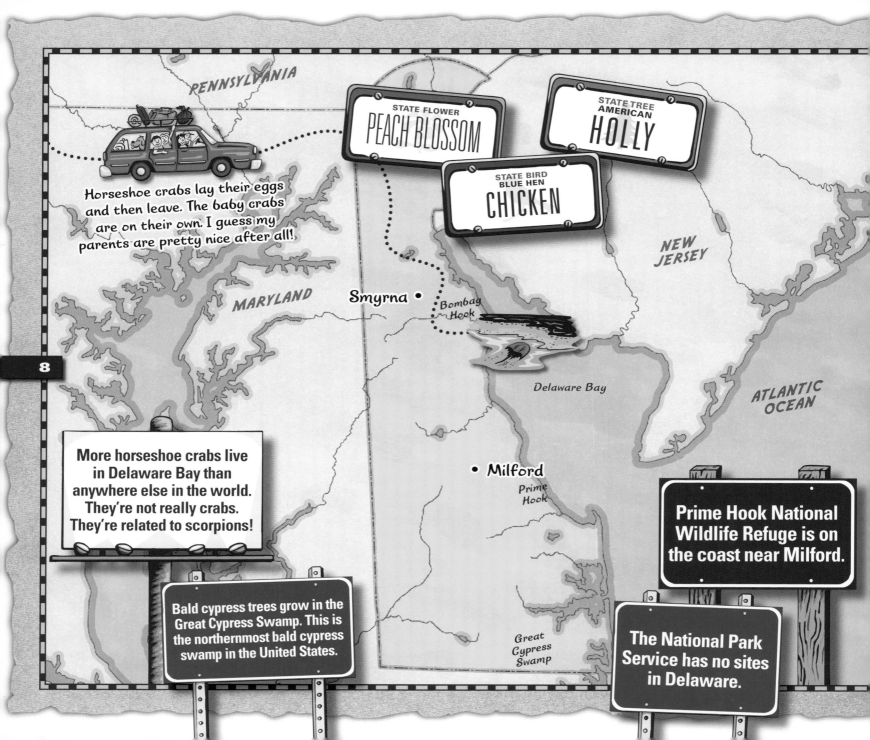

Horseshoe crabs lay their eggs and then leave. The baby crabs are on their own. I guess my parents are pretty nice after all!

STATE FLOWER
PEACH BLOSSOM

STATE TREE AMERICAN
HOLLY

STATE BIRD BLUE HEN
CHICKEN

PENNSYLVANIA

MARYLAND

NEW JERSEY

Smyrna •

Bombay Hook

Delaware Bay

ATLANTIC OCEAN

• Milford

Prime Hook

Great Cypress Swamp

More horseshoe crabs live in Delaware Bay than anywhere else in the world. They're not really crabs. They're related to scorpions!

Bald cypress trees grow in the Great Cypress Swamp. This is the northernmost bald cypress swamp in the United States.

Prime Hook National Wildlife Refuge is on the coast near Milford.

The National Park Service has no sites in Delaware.

Wildlife at Bombay Hook

This horseshoe crab calls Bombay Hook National Wildlife Refuge home.

Want to see some really interesting animals? Just visit Bombay Hook National Wildlife Refuge. It's on the coast east of Smyrna.

In May, thousands of horseshoe crabs come ashore. They lay their eggs in the sand. Millions of ducks and geese come here, too. Some spend the winter. Others stay awhile and then fly away. Still, more than 200 kinds of birds nest here.

Delaware's forests and fields are full of wildlife. You'll see foxes, moles, beavers, and deer. Off the coast are clams, crabs, and oysters. Snapping turtles live in the swamps. Don't stick your fingers in the water!

Canada geese and snow geese make their homes at Bombay Hook.

Bald eagles nest at Bombay Hook. They collect sticks to build their nests. They catch fish in the water to feed their young.

Want to learn more about Native American culture?
Head to the Nanticoke Indian Powwow!

People from the Netherlands are called Dutch people.

The Nanticoke Indian Powwow near Oak Orchard

Taste delicious **frybread** covered with powdered sugar. Hear tales of ancient **legends.** Watch swirling dancers in colorful feathers and beads. It's the Nanticoke Indian Powwow!

The Nanticoke once lived throughout the Delmarva Peninsula. They hunted and fished for food. They used clamshells as trade goods.

Dutch people settled in present-day Lewes in 1631. They named their settlement Zwaanendael. That means "valley of the swans." But conflicts broke out with local Indians. The Dutch **colony** lasted less than a year.

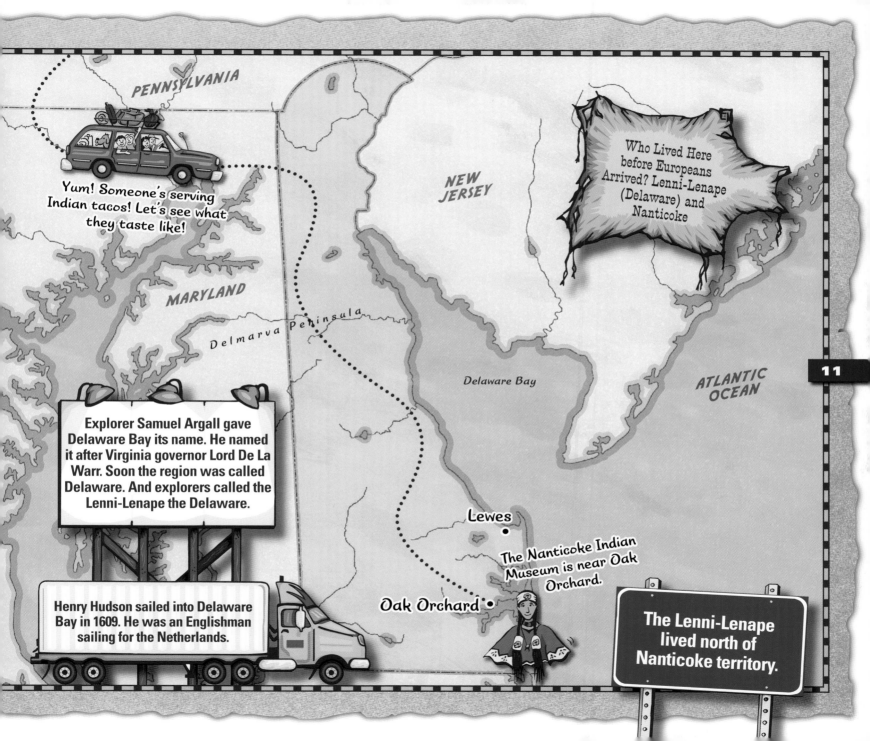

PENNSYLVANIA

Yum! Someone's serving Indian tacos! Let's see what they taste like!

NEW JERSEY

Who Lived Here before Europeans Arrived? Lenni-Lenape (Delaware) and Nanticoke

MARYLAND

Delmarva Peninsula

Delaware Bay

ATLANTIC OCEAN

Explorer Samuel Argall gave Delaware Bay its name. He named it after Virginia governor Lord De La Warr. Soon the region was called Delaware. And explorers called the Lenni-Lenape the Delaware.

Lewes

The Nanticoke Indian Museum is near Oak Orchard.

Oak Orchard

Henry Hudson sailed into Delaware Bay in 1609. He was an Englishman sailing for the Netherlands.

The Lenni-Lenape lived north of Nanticoke territory.

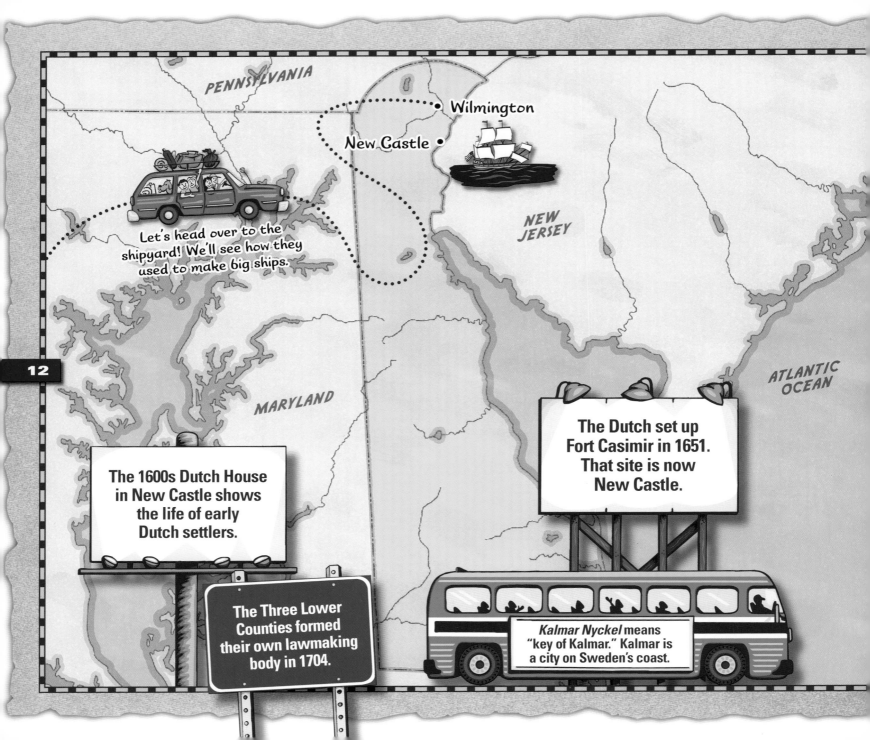

PENNSYLVANIA

Wilmington

New Castle

NEW JERSEY

ATLANTIC OCEAN

MARYLAND

Let's head over to the shipyard! We'll see how they used to make big ships.

The 1600s Dutch House in New Castle shows the life of early Dutch settlers.

The Three Lower Counties formed their own lawmaking body in 1704.

The Dutch set up Fort Casimir in 1651. That site is now New Castle.

Kalmar Nyckel means "key of Kalmar." Kalmar is a city on Sweden's coast.

Exploring the *Kalmar Nyckel*

Ahoy, mates! Climb aboard the *Kalmar Nyckel*. It's docked at Wilmington's harbor. You'll gaze up at its ten-story mast. Then you'll go below deck. You'll learn how passengers ate, slept, and played.

This ship is built like the original *Kalmar Nyckel*. It carried Swedish **colonists** here in 1638. They founded Fort Christina in present-day Wilmington. They named their colony New Sweden. This region fell under Dutch rule. Then England took over in 1664.

William Penn founded the Pennsylvania Colony in 1682. It included what is now Delaware. Delaware was called Pennsylvania's Three Lower Counties.

Try out your sea legs aboard the Kalmar Nyckel.

13

Want to learn about Delaware's capitol?
Just climb the steps of Legislative Hall.

Delaware has 3 counties—
New Castle, Kent, and
Sussex. They used to be
Pennsylvania Colony's
Three Lower Counties.

The State Capitol in Dover

Delaware's state capitol is called Legislative Hall. Why? Because legislation goes on there! Legislation means making laws. Delaware's lawmakers are members of the General Assembly.

Lawmaking is one branch of Delaware's state government. The government has two other branches. One branch carries out the laws. It's headed by the governor. The governor has offices in the capitol, too. Another branch is made up of state courts. Judges rule over these courts. They decide whether laws have been broken.

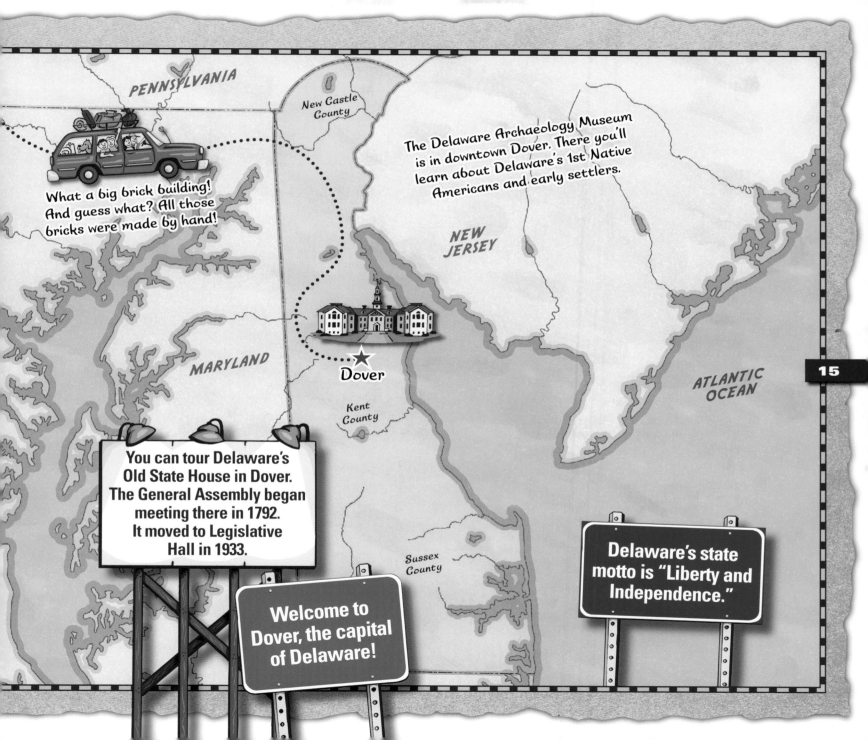

PENNSYLVANIA

What a big brick building! And guess what? All those bricks were made by hand!

New Castle County

The Delaware Archaeology Museum is in downtown Dover. There you'll learn about Delaware's 1st Native Americans and early settlers.

NEW JERSEY

MARYLAND

Dover

Kent County

ATLANTIC OCEAN

You can tour Delaware's Old State House in Dover. The General Assembly began meeting there in 1792. It moved to Legislative Hall in 1933.

Sussex County

Welcome to Dover, the capital of Delaware!

Delaware's state motto is "Liberty and Independence."

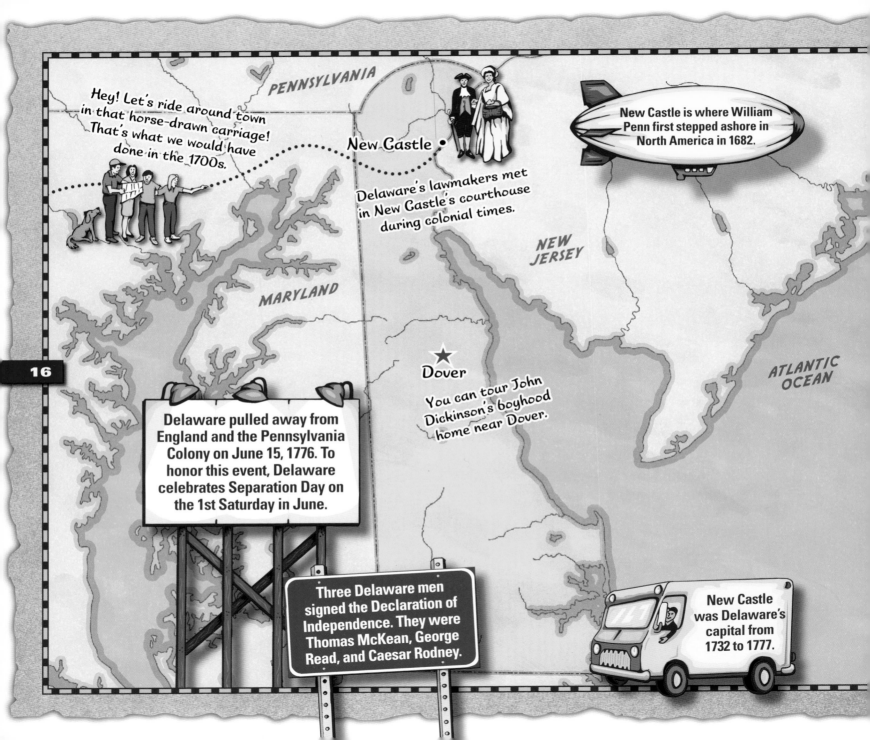

PENNSYLVANIA

Hey! Let's ride around town in that horse-drawn carriage! That's what we would have done in the 1700s.

New Castle

New Castle is where William Penn first stepped ashore in North America in 1682.

Delaware's lawmakers met in New Castle's courthouse during colonial times.

NEW JERSEY

MARYLAND

Dover

ATLANTIC OCEAN

You can tour John Dickinson's boyhood home near Dover.

Delaware pulled away from England and the Pennsylvania Colony on June 15, 1776. To honor this event, Delaware celebrates Separation Day on the 1st Saturday in June.

Three Delaware men signed the Declaration of Independence. They were Thomas McKean, George Read, and Caesar Rodney.

New Castle was Delaware's capital from 1732 to 1777.

A Day in Old New Castle

Soldiers fire their cannons. Ladies serve dainty cups of tea. Children dance around a maypole. And lots of people are dressed in 1700s clothing. You're enjoying a tour called A Day in Old New Castle! New Castle was Delaware's colonial capital.

The colonies wanted freedom from England. They fought the Revolutionary War (1775–1783) and won. The colonies then became the United States.

Colonial leaders met during the war. They wrote the Declaration of Independence in 1776. Later, they wrote the Constitution. It laid out the new nation's basic laws. Delaware was the first to approve the Constitution. Then it became the first state!

17

Getting dizzy? Discover fun games from the 1700s at A Day in Old New Castle.

John Dickinson and George Read helped write the Constitution. Dickinson was also from Delaware.

Fenwick Island's Shipwreck Museum

Look at all those sailboats! Delawareans can sail out to sea from this port in Lewes.

Imagine finding a long-lost treasure ship. It's filled with chests of coins and jewels. Gold and silver sparkle before your eyes.

You'll discover treasures like this on Fenwick Island. Just visit the DiscoverSea Shipwreck Museum!

This museum is devoted to sunken ships. It contains hundreds of fascinating objects. They were all recovered from shipwrecks. Each item has a story to tell!

Delaware has a long history with the sea. Its shipyards built huge sailing ships. Even today, Delaware is connected to the sea. Ocean ships sail in and out of Delaware Bay. Luckily, they rarely sink anymore!

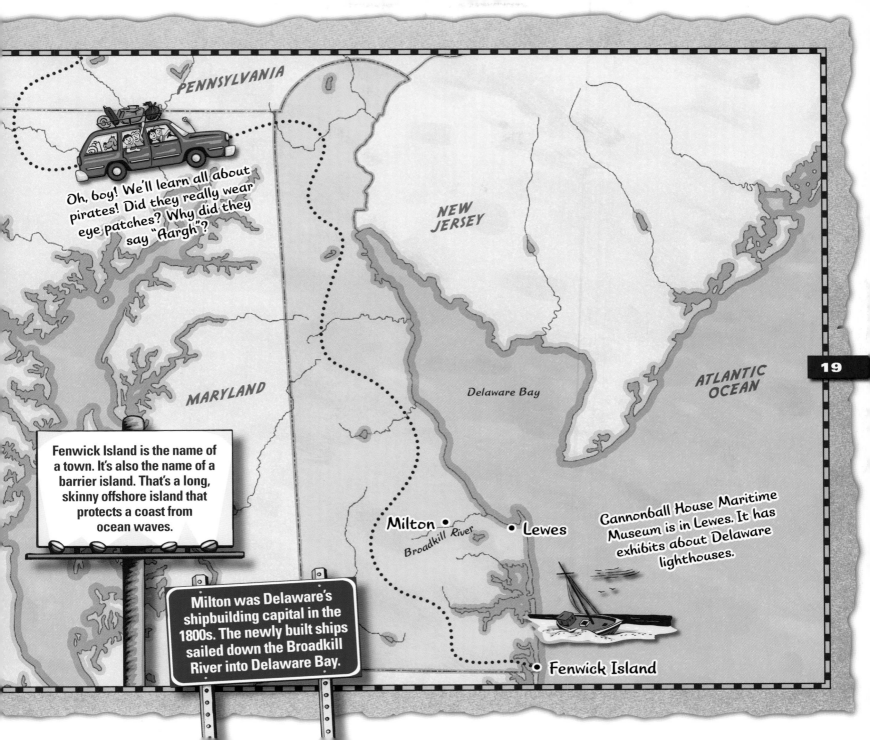

PENNSYLVANIA

Oh, boy! We'll learn all about pirates! Did they really wear eye patches? Why did they say "Aargh"?

NEW JERSEY

ATLANTIC OCEAN

MARYLAND

Delaware Bay

Fenwick Island is the name of a town. It's also the name of a barrier island. That's a long, skinny offshore island that protects a coast from ocean waves.

Milton • • Lewes
Broadkill River

Cannonball House Maritime Museum is in Lewes. It has exhibits about Delaware lighthouses.

Milton was Delaware's shipbuilding capital in the 1800s. The newly built ships sailed down the Broadkill River into Delaware Bay.

• Fenwick Island

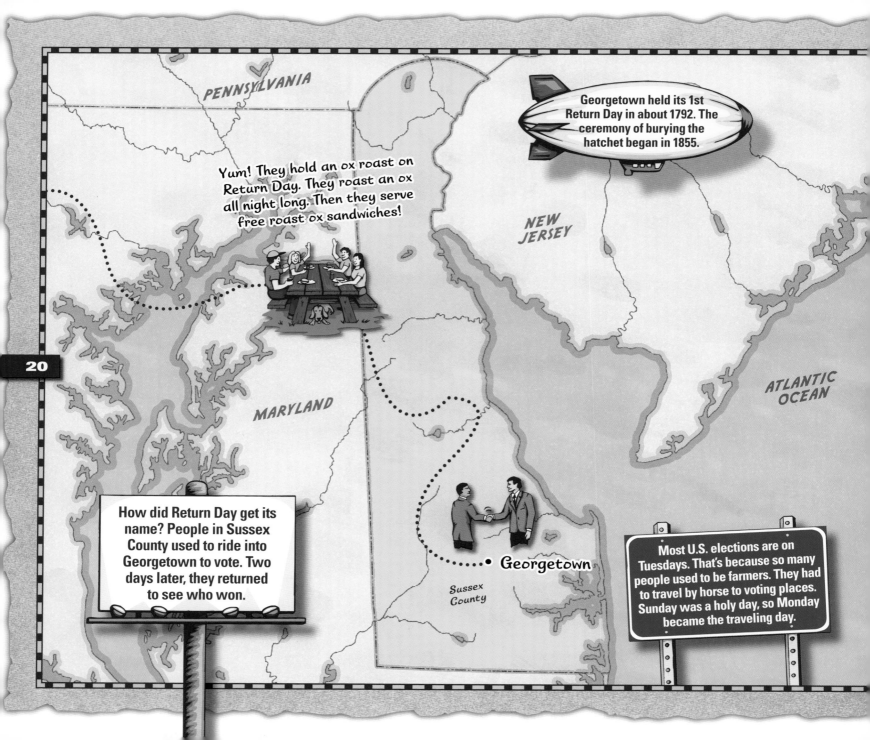

Burying the Hatchet in Georgetown

Did anyone ever tell you to bury the hatchet? That means to stop being enemies. Be friends instead!

This saying arose from a Native American ceremony. Two groups would meet and bury a hatchet. It was a sign that they were making peace.

Two rivals bury the hatchet on Return Day.

Georgetown follows this custom, too. It happens on Return Day. That's the Thursday after an election. The winner and loser meet and shake hands. They ride together in a horse-drawn carriage. Then, together, they bury a hatchet in the sand. No more hard feelings!

U.S. presidential elections take place on the 1st Tuesday after the 1st Monday in November.

How did farmers make flour without electricity? Visit Loockerman Landing Village to find out.

Dover's Agricultural Museum and Village

Explore the farmhouse. You'll see the wood-burning stove in the kitchen. Stop by the old water-powered mill. That's where grain was ground up. Then duck into the henhouse. Kids used to gather eggs there.

You're touring Loockerman Landing Village! It's part of the Delaware Agricultural Museum and Village. There you see how Delaware farmers once lived.

The new state of Delaware had rich soil. Lots of people moved there to farm. They raised cows, chickens, hogs, and sheep. Many grew wheat and corn. They ground wheat into flour at **gristmills.** Delaware became the top flour-milling state.

Blacksmiths in the 1800s made nails, horseshoes, cooking tools, and many other useful items.

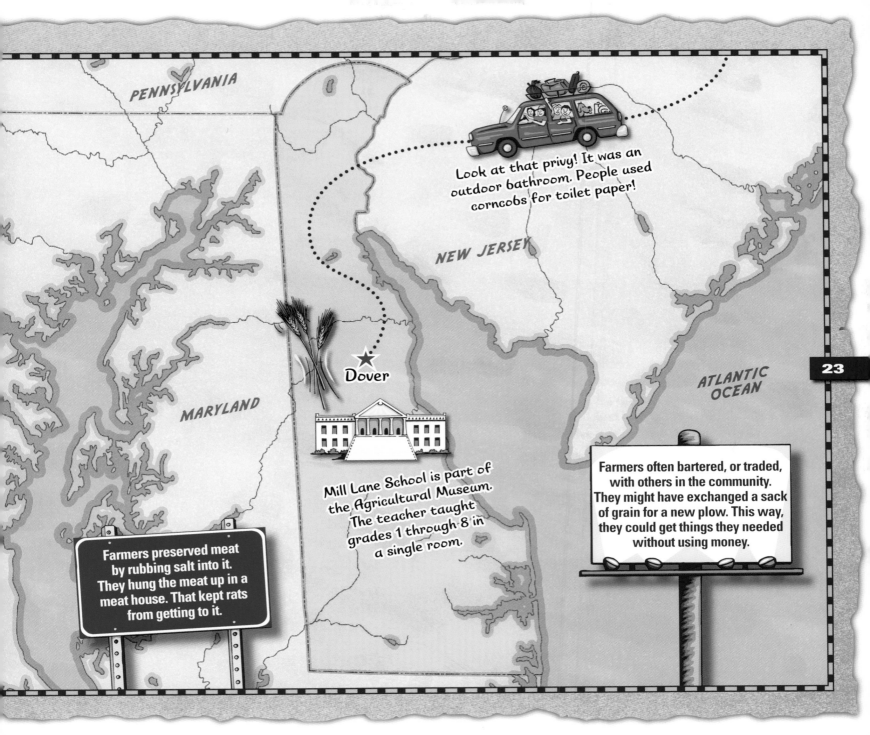

Look at that privy! It was an outdoor bathroom. People used corncobs for toilet paper!

PENNSYLVANIA

NEW JERSEY

MARYLAND

★ Dover

ATLANTIC OCEAN

Mill Lane School is part of the Agricultural Museum. The teacher taught grades 1 through 8 in a single room.

Farmers preserved meat by rubbing salt into it. They hung the meat up in a meat house. That kept rats from getting to it.

Farmers often bartered, or traded, with others in the community. They might have exchanged a sack of grain for a new plow. This way, they could get things they needed without using money.

PENNSYLVANIA

I've got to see that giant frying pan. My bed and Sparky's doghouse would both fit inside it!

Delaware's Sussex County is the nation's top chicken-producing county. For every person in Sussex County, there are more than 1,300 chickens!

NEW JERSEY

ATLANTIC OCEAN

Cecile Steele of Ocean View developed Delaware's broiler **industry** in 1923. Her broiler house is now at the Delaware Agricultural Museum in Dover.

★ Dover

Harrington •

The state fair is held in Harrington in July each year.

• Milford

What Are Delaware's Fishing Products? Crabs, clams, and sea bass

Sussex County

Millsboro •

• Ocean View

What Does Delaware Raise? Broilers (chickens), milk, and soybeans

The Delmarva Chicken Festival

Peep, peep! Look at the baby chicks. They're so soft and fluffy!

You're at the Delmarva Chicken Festival! A different town hosts this festival every year. Sometimes it's in Delaware, and sometimes it's in Maryland. Dover, Milford, and Millsboro have all been hosts.

Chickens are a big deal in Delaware. Delaware is a top state for producing broilers. They're chickens that are five to twelve weeks old. Broilers are Delaware's leading farm product. Lots of farmers raise dairy cows, too. Soybeans and corn are Delaware's major crops.

Want to hold a little chick? Be sure to stop by the Delmarva Chicken Festival.

A giant frying pan was made for the 1950 Delmarva Chicken Festival. The pan measures 10 feet (3 m) across. It can cook 200 chickens at once!

Many mills in Delaware were once powered by water. Watch the big wheel turn!

Éleuthère Irénée du Pont's family members ran his company after he died.

Stroll through the mill workers' village. Watch the massive waterwheel turning. Then try on a modern space suit!

You're visiting Hagley Museum. It shows how Delaware's early factories worked.

Éleuthère Irénée du Pont built a gunpowder mill here. It was right by Brandywine Creek. Many other mills stood along this creek. The water turned their big mill wheels. The wheels made the mills' machines work. The mills made paper, lumber, cloth, and other goods.

Du Pont built his mill in 1802. He became the country's biggest gunpowder maker. His business grew into the DuPont company. It's Delaware's largest company today.

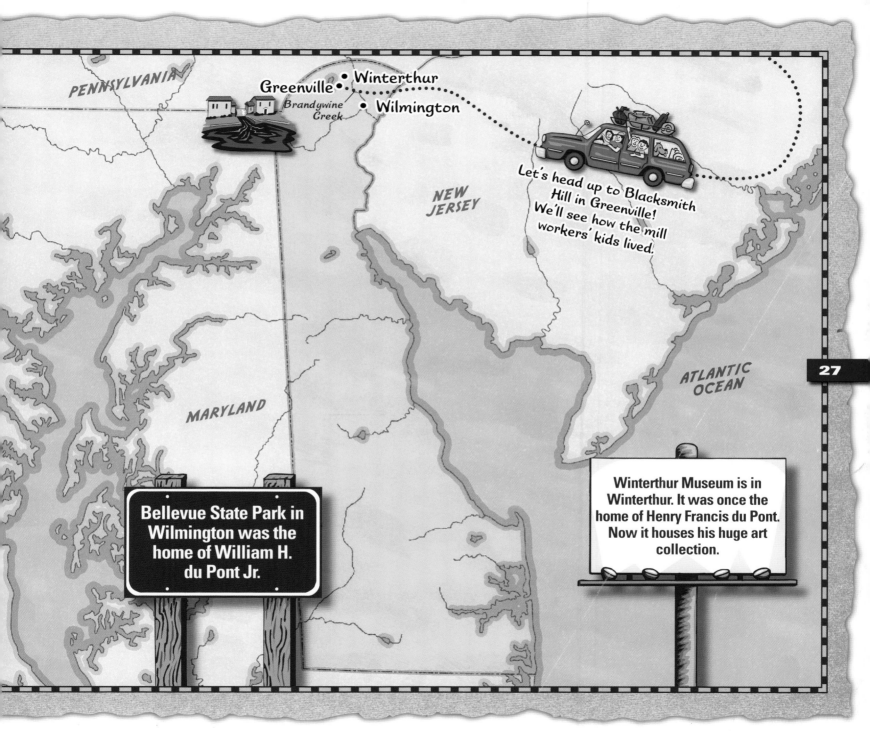

PENNSYLVANIA

Greenville • Winterthur

Brandywine Creek

• Wilmington

NEW JERSEY

Let's head up to Blacksmith Hill in Greenville! We'll see how the mill workers' kids lived!

MARYLAND

ATLANTIC OCEAN

Bellevue State Park in Wilmington was the home of William H. du Pont Jr.

Winterthur Museum is in Winterthur. It was once the home of Henry Francis du Pont. Now it houses his huge art collection.

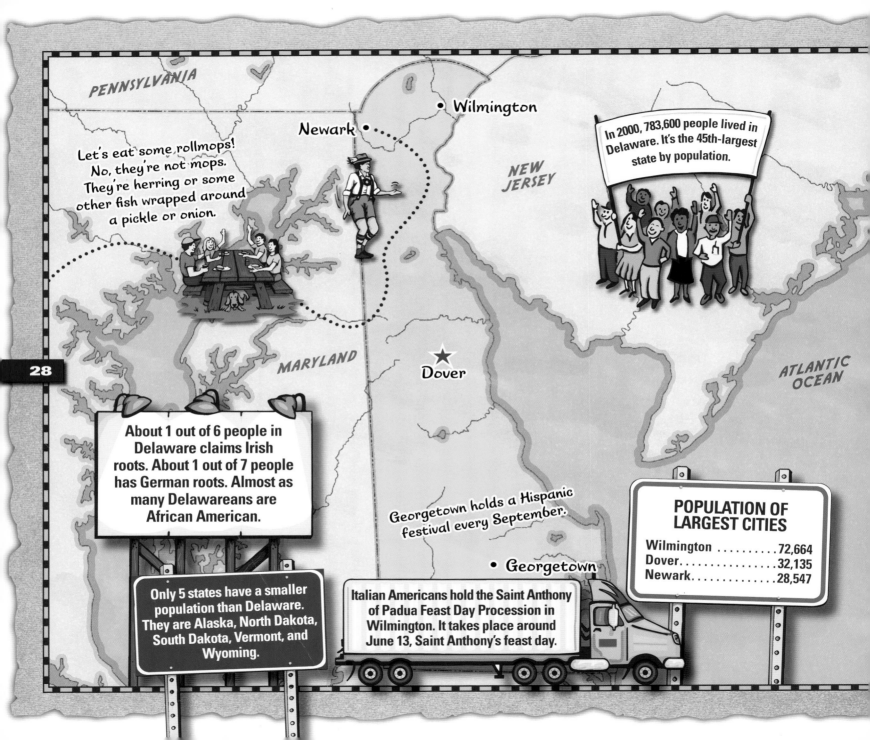

PENNSYLVANIA

• Wilmington

Newark •

Let's eat some rollmops! No, they're not mops. They're herring or some other fish wrapped around a pickle or onion.

NEW JERSEY

In 2000, 783,600 people lived in Delaware. It's the 45th-largest state by population.

MARYLAND

★ Dover

ATLANTIC OCEAN

About 1 out of 6 people in Delaware claims Irish roots. About 1 out of 7 people has German roots. Almost as many Delawareans are African American.

Georgetown holds a Hispanic festival every September.

POPULATION OF LARGEST CITIES

Wilmington 72,664
Dover. 32,135
Newark. 28,547

Only 5 states have a smaller population than Delaware. They are Alaska, North Dakota, South Dakota, Vermont, and Wyoming.

• Georgetown

Italian Americans hold the Saint Anthony of Padua Feast Day Procession in Wilmington. It takes place around June 13, Saint Anthony's feast day.

Oktoberfest in Newark

Munch on some pretzels and bratwurst. Then watch the dancers. The men are wearing *lederhosen*. And women are wearing *dirndls*. These are **traditional** German costumes.

It's time for Oktoberfest! Newark holds this big German festival every year.

Many German **immigrants** settled in Delaware. They worked in the state's mills and factories. Others came from Ireland, Italy, or Greece. Some left homelands in England, Poland, or Asia. And some came from Mexico and other Spanish-speaking lands.

Many of Delaware's African Americans are descended from slaves. After the Civil War (1861–1865), all slaves were freed.

Want to learn about German culture? Watch the dancers whirl at Oktoberfest.

Oktoberfests are usually held in October. But Newark's Oktoberfest is in September. The weather is warmer then!

A Day at the Beach with DuPont

How about a day at the beach? Head on out to Cape Henlopen State Park. The DuPont company is nowhere in sight. But its products are!

Your bathing suit might be made of nylon. If it's stretchy, it's probably Lycra. Maybe you're reading a book. Is its cover waterproof? It could be made of Tyvek.

DuPont invented nylon, Lycra, and Tyvek. Its Experimental Station in Wilmington opened in 1903. Scientists there developed many new materials.

Today, banking companies employ the most Delaware workers. But DuPont is still one of Delaware's largest employers.

Do you like the beach? Don't forget to go to Cape Henlopen State Park.

DuPont sold a lot of ammunition to the U.S. government during World War I (1914–1918).

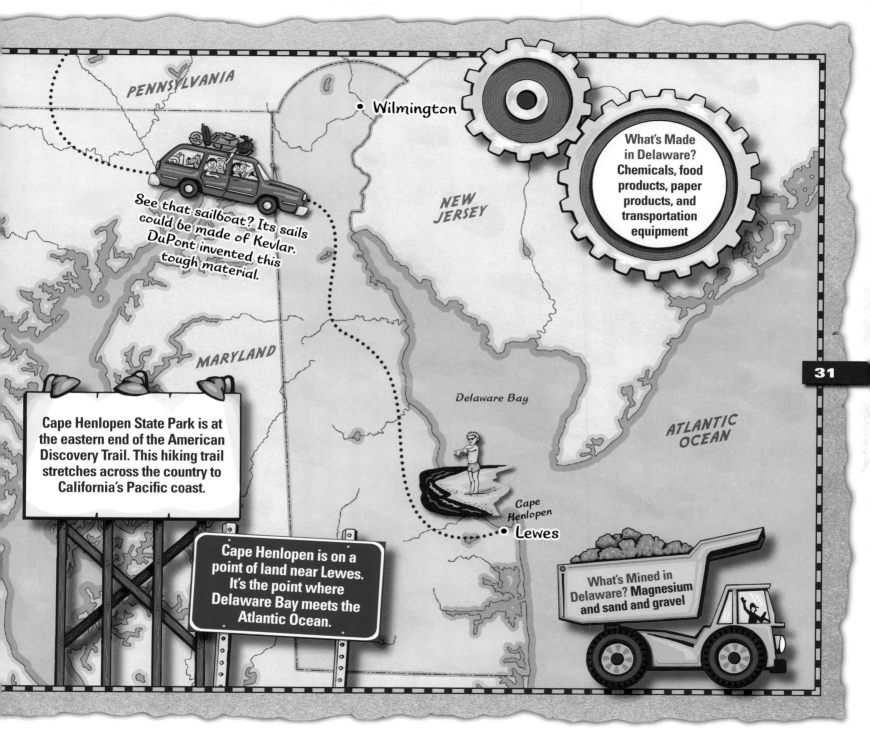

PENNSYLVANIA

• Wilmington

NEW JERSEY

What's Made in Delaware? Chemicals, food products, paper products, and transportation equipment

See that sailboat? Its sails could be made of Kevlar. DuPont invented this tough material.

MARYLAND

Delaware Bay

ATLANTIC OCEAN

Cape Henlopen State Park is at the eastern end of the American Discovery Trail. This hiking trail stretches across the country to California's Pacific coast.

Cape Henlopen

Cape Henlopen is on a point of land near Lewes. It's the point where Delaware Bay meets the Atlantic Ocean.

• Lewes

What's Mined in Delaware? Magnesium and sand and gravel

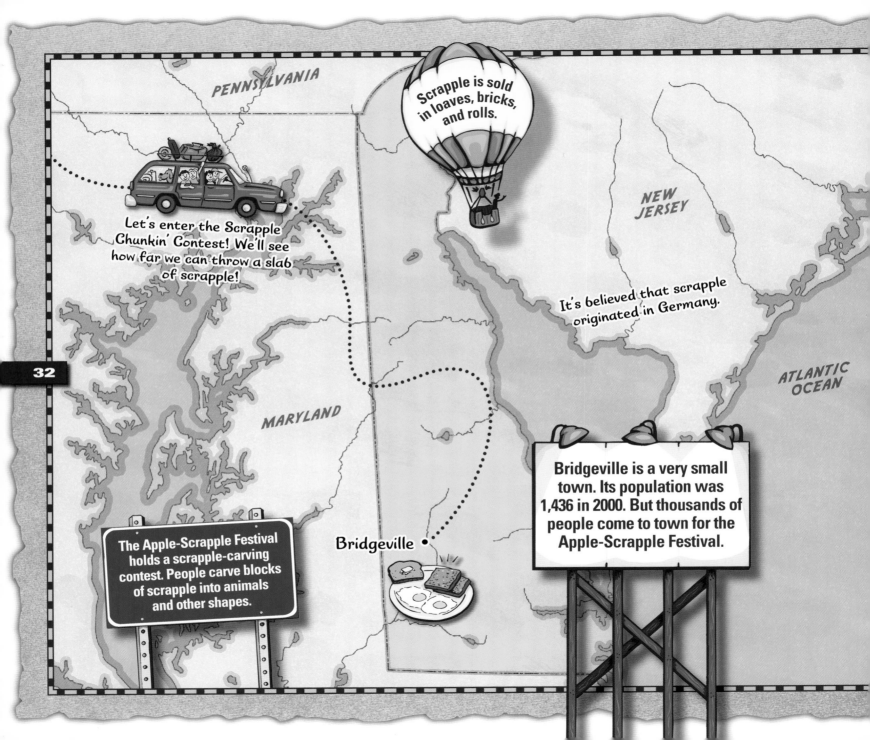

PENNSYLVANIA

Scrapple is sold in loaves, bricks, and rolls.

NEW JERSEY

Let's enter the Scrapple Chunkin' Contest! We'll see how far we can throw a slab of scrapple!

It's believed that scrapple originated in Germany.

32

MARYLAND

ATLANTIC OCEAN

The Apple-Scrapple Festival holds a scrapple-carving contest. People carve blocks of scrapple into animals and other shapes.

Bridgeville

Bridgeville is a very small town. Its population was 1,436 in 2000. But thousands of people come to town for the Apple-Scrapple Festival.

Bridgeville's Apple-Scrapple Festival

Apples and scrapple don't usually go together. But they do in Bridgeville. Just check out the Apple-Scrapple Festival!

What is scrapple? It's sort of like sausage. It's ground hog parts mixed with cornmeal. You mash it into a mold. Next, you slice it up. Then you fry it till it's crispy! People like to eat scrapple for breakfast.

The country's largest scrapple company is in Bridgeville. An apple-packing company is there, too. Put them together, and what have you got? The Apple-Scrapple Festival!

Ever tried scrapple before? Head to Bridgeville and have a taste!

At the Apple-Scrapple Festival, you can eat apple pie, candied apples, apple fritters, and apple dumplings.

Watch out for flying pumpkins! Things can get crazy at the Punkin Chunkin.

The Great Delaware Kite Festival is held at Cape Henlopen.

The Punkin Chunkin in Millsboro

S plat! A pumpkin smashes into a tree. Fwap! A pumpkin lands in the woods. It's the World Championship Punkin Chunkin!

Teams of people bring big machines here. They use the machines to hurl the pumpkins. Whoever's pumpkin travels the farthest wins!

The Punkin Chunkin is a famous event. But Delaware offers many ways to have fun. Lots of people enjoy the outdoors. They go swimming and boating along the coast. Or they camp and hike in the forests.

How about you? Would you rather take a hike? Or would you rather watch the Punkin Chunkin?

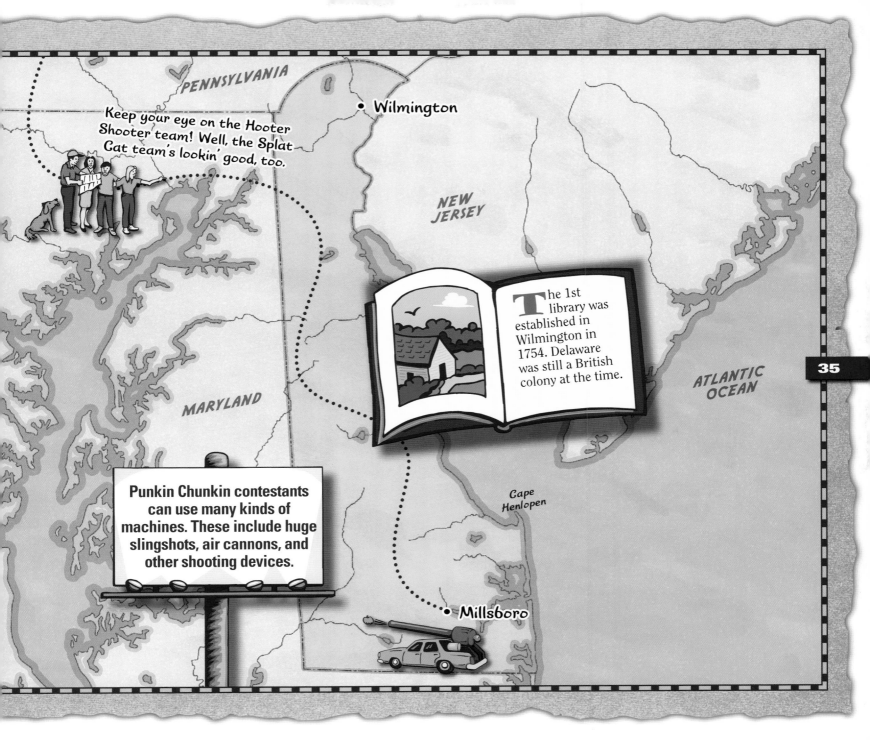

Keep your eye on the Hooter Shooter team! Well, the Splat Cat team's lookin' good, too.

PENNSYLVANIA

• Wilmington

NEW JERSEY

The 1st library was established in Wilmington in 1754. Delaware was still a British colony at the time.

MARYLAND

ATLANTIC OCEAN

Cape Henlopen

Punkin Chunkin contestants can use many kinds of machines. These include huge slingshots, air cannons, and other shooting devices.

• Millsboro

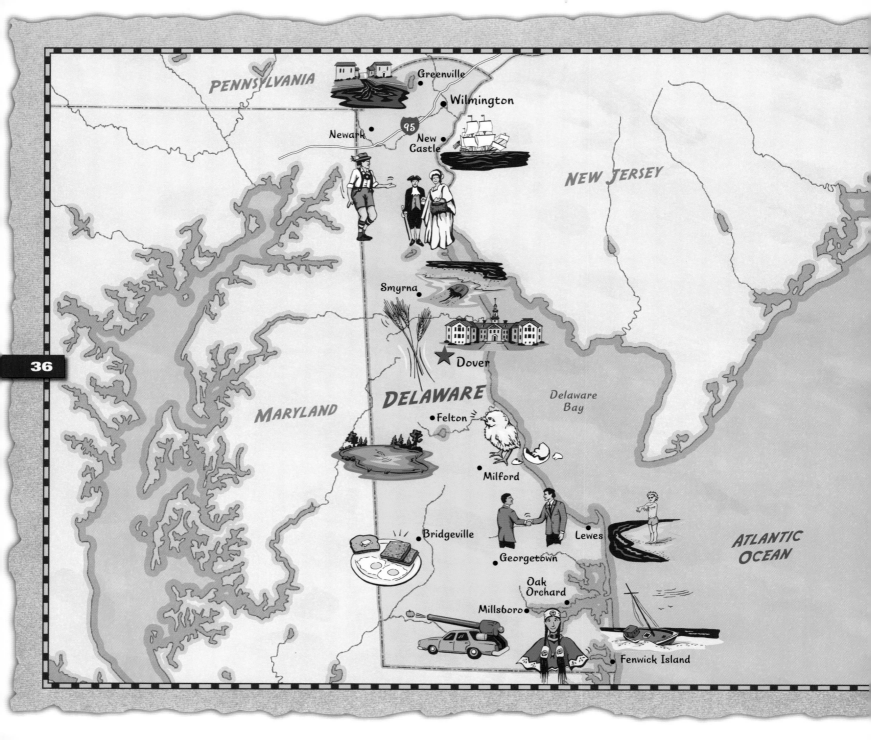

PENNSYLVANIA

Greenville

Wilmington

Newark

95

New
Castle

NEW JERSEY

Smyrna

Dover

MARYLAND

DELAWARE

Delaware
Bay

Felton

Milford

Bridgeville

Georgetown

Lewes

ATLANTIC
OCEAN

Oak
Orchard

Millsboro

Fenwick Island

OUR TRIP

We visited many amazing places on our trip! We also met a lot of interesting people along the way. Look at the map on the left. Use your finger to trace all the places we have been.

What state is smaller than Delaware? See page 6 for the answer.

What are people from the Netherlands called? Page 10 has the answer.

How many colonies did England establish along the Atlantic Coast? See page 13 for the answer.

What was Delaware's capital from 1732 to 1777? Look on page 16 for the answer.

How did farmers preserve meat? Page 23 has the answer.

Who developed Delaware's broiler industry? Turn to page 24 for the answer.

What's a rollmop? Look on page 28 for the answer.

Where is the Great Delaware Kite Festival held? Turn to page 34 for the answer.

That was a great trip! We have traveled all over Delaware!

There are a few places that we didn't have time for, though. Next time, we plan to visit Abbott's Mill Nature Center in Milton. Visitors can hike various trails through scenic woods and fields. If there's time, they can even visit a historic gristmill!

More Places to Visit in Delaware

WORDS TO KNOW

colonists (KOL-uh-nists) people who settle a new land for their home country

colony (KOL-uh-nee) a territory settled and ruled by another country

frybread (FRY-bred) a deep-fried bread made by Native Americans

gristmills (GRIHST-mihlz) mills for grinding grain

immigrants (IM-uh-gruhnts) people who leave their home country and move to another country

industry (IN-duh-stree) a type of business

legends (LEJ-undz) stories created to explain mysteries or teach lessons

peninsula (puh-NIN-soo-luh) a piece of land almost completely surrounded by water

traditional (truh-DISH-uhn-uhl) following long-held customs

Delaware covers 1,954 square miles (5,060 sq km). It's the 49th-largest state in size.

STATE SYMBOLS

State beverage: Milk

State bird: Blue hen chicken

State butterfly: Tiger swallowtail

State fish: Weakfish (sea trout)

State flower: Peach blossom

State fossil: Belemnite

State herb: Sweet golden rod

State insect: Ladybug

State marine animal: Horseshoe crab

State mineral: Sillimanite

State tree: American holly

State flag

State seal

STATE SONG

"Our Delaware"

Words by George B. Hynson (verses 1–3) and Donn Devine (verse 4),
music by William M. S. Brown

Oh the hills of dear New Castle,
And the smiling vales between,
When the corn is all in tassel,
And the meadowlands are green;
Where the cattle crop the clover,
And its breath is in the air,
While the sun is shining over
Our beloved Delaware.

Chorus:
Oh our Delaware!
Our beloved Delaware!
For the sun is shining over
Our beloved Delaware,
Oh our Delaware,
Our beloved Delaware!
Here's the loyal son that pledges,
Faith to good old Delaware.

Where the wheat fields break
    and billow,
In the peaceful land of Kent,
Where the toiler seeks his pillow,
With the blessings of content;
Where the bloom that tints the
    peaches,
Cheeks of merry maidens share,
And the woodland chorus preaches
A rejoicing Delaware.

(Chorus)

Dear old Sussex visions linger,
Of the holly and the pine,
Of Henlopen's Jeweled finger,
Flashing out across the brine;
Of the gardens and the hedges,
And the welcome waiting there,
For the loyal son that pledges
Faith to good old Delaware.

(Chorus)

From New Castle's rolling meadows,
Through the fair rich fields of Kent,
To the Sussex shores hear echoes,
Of the pledge we now present;
Liberty and Independence,
We will guard with loyal care,
And hold fast to freedom's presence,
In our home state Delaware.

FAMOUS PEOPLE

Allen, Richard (1760–1831), religious leader

Bayard, James Asheton (1767–1815), lawyer and statesman

Bird, Robert Montgomery (1806–1854), playwright and novelist

Canby, Henry Seidel (1878–1961), editor and critic

Cannon, Annie Jump (1863–1941), astronomer

Clayton, John Middleton (1796–1856), statesman

Darley, Felix (1822–1888), illustrator

duPont, Éleuthère Irénée (1771–1834), founder of DuPont Company

duPont, Pierre Samuel (1870–1954), businessman

Heimlich, Henry Jay (1920–), surgeon and inventor

Johnson, "Judy" (1899–1989), baseball player

Jones, Jacob (1768–1850), naval officer and war hero

Marquand, J. P. (1893–1960), novelist

Phillippe, Ryan (1974–), actor

Pyle, Howard (1853–1911), author and illustrator

Read, George (1733–1798), patriot during the American Revolution

Redding, Louis (1901–1999), Delaware's 1st African American lawyer

Rodney, Caesar (1728–1784), patriot during the American Revolution

Shue, Elisabeth (1963–), actor

White, Randy (1953–), football player

TO FIND OUT MORE

At the Library
Blashfield, Jean F. *The Delaware Colony*. Chanhassen, Minn.: The Child's World, 2004.

Crane, Carol, and Elizabeth Traynor (illustrator). *F Is for First State: A Delaware Alphabet*. Chelsea, Mich.: Sleeping Bear Press, 2004.

Mitchell, Barbara, and Todd L. W. Doney (illustrator). *Red Bird*. New York: Lothrop, Lee & Shepard Books, 1996.

Pyle, Howard. *The Book of Pirates*. Mineola, N.Y.: Dover Publications, 2000.

Wiener, Roberta, and James R. Arnold. *Delaware*. Chicago: Raintree, 2004.

On the Web
Visit our home page for lots of links about Delaware:
http://www.childsworld.com/links
Note to Parents, Teachers, and Librarians: We routinely verify our Web links to make sure they are safe, active sites—so encourage your readers to check them out!

Places to Visit or Contact
Delaware Tourism Office
99 Kings Highway
Dover, DE 19901
866/284-7483
For more information about traveling in Delaware

The Historical Society of Delaware
505 Market Street
Wilmington, DE 19801
302/655-7161
For more information about the history of Delaware

INDEX

Bye, First State.
We had a great time.
We'll come back soon!